100 HADITHS

FOR CHILDREN

Erol Ergün

Copyright © 2013 by Tughra Books

Originally published in Turkish as *100 Hadis* in 2008

20 19 18 17   2 3 4 5

Translated by Ebru Erginbaş

Published by Tughra Books
345 Clifton Ave., Clifton,
NJ, 07011, USA

www.tughrabooks.com

Library of Congress Cataloging-in-Publication Data Available

ISBN: 978-1-59784-320-1

Printed by
Çağlayan A.Ş., Izmir - Turkey

Contents

Etiquette...5

Daily Life.......................................41

Worship 71

Knowledge....................................83

Charity and Compassion...............93

"May Allah brighten the face of a person who hears something from us and reports it to others without altering it. There are many people who better understand and conserve the knowledge than the person who first heard it."

(*Sunan at-Tirmidhi*, Ilm, 7)

Etiquette

1

A smile is charity.

2

Greet one another
(by saying, As-salamu
alaikum).

3

A kind word is charity.

4

Show mercy to others
and you will be treated
with mercy.

9

5

It is enough sin for a person to speak everything that he hears.

6

If you put down
someone for their actions,
one day you will act the
same way.

7

Islam is good manners.

8

Act righteously, because righteousness leads to good behavior, and good behavior leads to Paradise.

9

Beware of telling lies, for lying leads to immorality and immorality leads to Hellfire.

10

The best person is the one
who has good manners.

11

When you begin eating, say, Bismillah. Eat with your right hand and eat what is in front of you.

12

Allah does not judge you according to your bodies and appearances, but He looks into your hearts and observes your deeds.

13

Whoever believes in Allah
and the Last Day should
speak good things or keep
silent.

14

The one who engages in
malicious gossip will not enter
Paradise unless he is either
punished or forgiven.

This is one of the Prophetic sayings that people know: "Do whatever you like to do, if you were not ashamed."

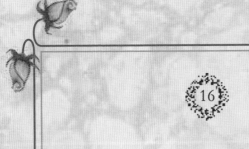

16

Cleanliness is half of faith.

One who observes economy does not suffer shortage in livelihood for their family.

18

One who consults will not
have cause to regret.

19

The stingiest person is the one who does not greet his brother or sister when he or she sees them.

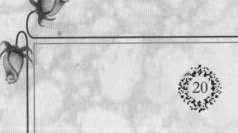

Do not judge a person while you are angry.

Do not be envious of others, because envy burns good deeds like fire burns wood.

22

Be careful of suspicion, for it is the most mistaken of all speech. Do not spread the secrets of others, and do not look for a person's faults.

Gossip is saying something about a person that they would not be happy to hear. If your words are true, it is gossip, but if your words are not true, it is slander.

24

If you believe in Allah,
you should be kind to people
and love them for His sake.

29

Be careful who you spend your time with, because a person will be like his or her friends.

26

If you are in a group of three, two of you should not whisper to one another and leave the third person out.

If someone avoids arguing while he is wrong, he will have a home on the edge of Paradise. If he avoids it while he is right, he will have a home in the middle of Paradise.

28

It is not good manners to
sit between two people without
their permission.

A believer is a person who
gets along well with others.
There is no good in a person
who has no kindness.

30

Do not make fun of another person's problems, because one day Allah may test you with the same problem.

31

If someone invites you, you should accept his or her invitation.

A Muslim has six
obligations to another
Muslim: to greet another
Muslim when you meet him;
to respond when he invites you;
to give him your (sincerest)
advice when he seeks it; to
say Yarhamuk Allah
when he sneezes and says
Alhamdulillah; to visit him
when he falls ill; and when he
dies, to attend his funeral.

Eat together and not separately, for the blessings is associated with the company.

34

A person is not a true believer until he wishes for another what he wishes for himself.

35

Allah treats people with compassion, so He loves people being compassionate with one another.

Daily

Life

One of the beautiful things about Islam is that it encourages people to stay away from things that are not important.

37

Be good to your mother,
because Paradise is
located at her feet.

38

Allah is pleased when
our parents are happy, and
Allah is angry when our
parents are angry.

There are three prayers
that are always accepted: the
prayer of the oppressed, the
prayer of the traveler, and
the prayer of the parents.

40

The Prayer at its appointed hour is the most beloved deed to Allah, and then treating your parents with kindness.

A person asked Allah's Messenger, "Who amongst the people is most deserving of my good treatment?" He said: "Your mother, again your mother, again your mother, then your father, then your nearest relatives according to the order (of nearness)."

42

By his good character
a believer will attain the
degree of one who prays
during the night and fasts
during the day.

43

If you want to live a long life filled with blessings, you must be kind to your parents and visit your family members.

It is a sin to insult your
brother or sister in Islam.

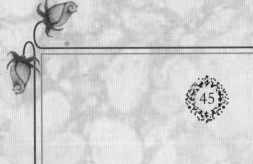

45

Contentment is an inexhaustible treasure.

Facilitate things to people (concerning religious matters), and do not make it hard for them and give them good tidings and do not make them run away (from Islam).

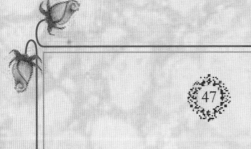

The intention of the
believer is more valuable
than his action.

48

Believers should show
mercy to those who are young
and respect to the elderly.

*He who deceives us
is not of us.*

*Keep good company,
because a person will be
with whom he loves.*

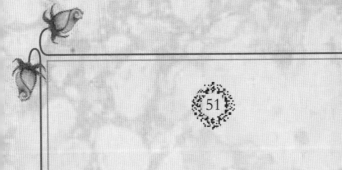

51

Patience is half of faith.

A believer is the mirror
of another believer.

53

There are two blessings
that people take for granted:
health and spare time.

54

Allah is pleased with people who complete their work and do it well.

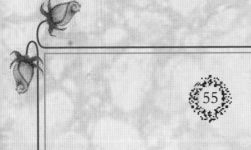

55

Do not harm others, even
if you are harmed first.

A Muslim is a person
whose hands and words
make everyone feel safe.

Muslims are brothers
and sisters to one another.
They do not harm one another
or let others harm their
fellow Muslims.

Believers are like a firm and solid structure.

59

Allah created a cure for all illnesses.

*Tie your camel safely,
and then trust it in
Allah's care.*

61

The most beloved of deeds to Allah are the ones that are continuous even if they are little.

Be moderate when you love someone, because someday they may turn into an enemy. Be moderate when you criticize your enemy, because someday they may turn into a friend.

63

Fear Allah wherever you are. Do good deeds after you sin, so that Allah may forgive your sins.

64

Treat people with kindness.

Worship

The prescribed Prayer
is the most important part
of religion.

66

The best person is one
who learns the Qur'an and
teaches it to others.

Everyone makes mistakes. The best person is the one who seeks forgiveness after making a mistake.

68

The prescribed Prayer
is the light of a believer.

The key to Paradise is saying, "La ilaha illallah" (There is no deity but Allah).

If there was a river passing by your home and you took a bath in it five times a day, would there be any dirt on you? Praying five times a day is like bathing in that river.

71

If anyone invokes blessings upon me once, Allah will bestow blessings upon him ten times over.

72

The most virtuous charity
is that you satisfy a hungry
stomach.

*The Daily Prayers
are the best deed.*

74

Whoever recites the Qur'an, memorizes it, and puts what is allowed and what is forbidden in it into practice, Allah will allow him or her to intercede for ten people from his or her family on the Day of Judgment.

Sleeping in the morning
leads to less sustenance.

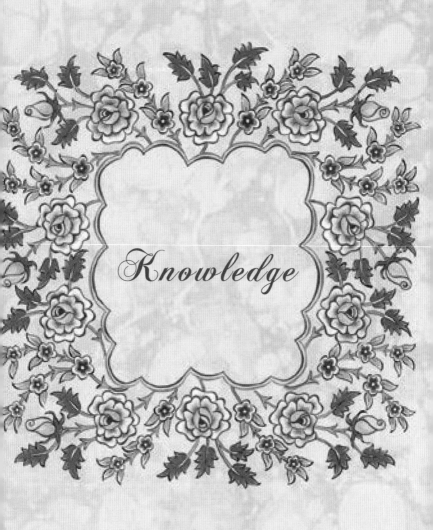

Knowledge

*If Allah wants to
do good to a person, He
makes him comprehend
the religion.*

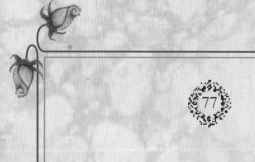

*Asking good questions
is part of learning.*

Seeking knowledge is required for all Muslims.

*Allah will make
the path to Paradise easy
for the person who seeks
knowledge.*

You should be a scholar,
or a student, or a listener,
or a lover of knowledge and
scholars, and you should
not be someone else.

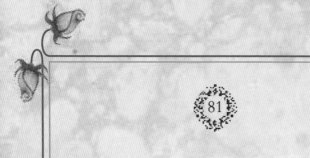

81

Knowledge makes up for past sins.

82

When you see a learning
circle, join it, because learning
circles are like gardens of
Paradise.

83

The best charity for a
Muslim is to learn and
then teach others the
knowledge.

If a person learns and then acts upon their knowledge, Allah will teach them more.

Charity

and

Compassion

If a person helps a believer
in this world, Allah will help
them in the Hereafter.

86

A Muslim does
not go to sleep with a full
stomach while knowing that
his or her neighbor
is hungry.

87

It is better to be uneducated and generous than to be knowledgeable and stingy.

88

A generous person is close to Allah and Paradise, while a greedy person is far from Allah and is close to Hellfire.

The believer is simple and generous, but the profligate is deceitful and ignoble.

90

*Act quickly to do
good deeds.*

It is not permissible for a Muslim to have estranged relations with his brother beyond three nights, the one turning one way and the other turning the other way when they meet; the better of the two is one who is the first to give a greeting.

Give gifts to each other
to strengthen the friendship
between you.

If a person causes a good deed to be done, he will be rewarded as if he had performed the good deed himself.

There are three signs
of a hypocrite: whenever he
speaks, he lies; whenever he
makes a promise, he breaks
it; and whenever he is trusted,
he betrays his trust.

When you visit someone who is sick, tell them good things about their lifespan and illness. Although your words may not heal them, they will make the person feel better.

96

Allah will not show mercy
to a person who shows no
mercy to people.

Show mercy to the creatures of the Earth so that Allah will show mercy to you.

98

Whoever shows respect
to an elderly person, Allah
will create for him in his
old-age someone who will
show him respect, too.

Don't bear aversion against one another and don't be jealous of one another and be servants of Allah.

*It is charity for a
Muslim to plant a tree
that people and animals
may eat from.*

THE REFERENCES FOR THE *HADITH*S

1. *Sunan at-Tirmidhi*, Birr, 36
2. *Sahih Muslim*, Iman, 93
3. *Sunan Abu Dawud*, Adab, 34
4. Tabarani, *Al-Mujamul Kabir*,
5. *Sunan Abu Dawud*, Adab, 80
6. *Sunan at-Tirmidhi*, Qiyama, 53
7. *Kanz al-Ummal*, 3/17
8. *Sunan Abu Dawud*, Adab, 69
9. *Sunan Abu Dawud*, Adab, 69
10. *Sahih al-Bukhari*, Manaqib, 23
11. *Sahih Muslim*, Aşriba, 105–106
12. *Sahih Muslim*, Birr, 33
13. *Sahih al-Bukhari*, Adab, 31
14. *Sahih Muslim*, Iman, 168
15. *Sahih al-Bukhari*, Anbiya, 54
16. *Sahih Muslim*, Taharat, 1
17. Tabarani, *Al-Mujamul Kabir*, 10/108
18. Tabarani, *Al-Mujamul Kabir*, 10/108
19. Tabarani, *Al-Mujamul Kabir*, 556
20. *Sunan Abu Dawud*, Aqdiya, 9
21. *Sunan Abu Dawud*, Adab, 52
22. *Sunan Abu Dawud*, Adab, 57–58
23. *Sahih Muslim*, Birr, 70
24. Tabarani, *Al-Mujamus-Saghir*, 2/21
25. *Sunan at-Tirmidhi*, Zuhd, 45
26. *Sahih Muslim*, Salam, 4053
27. *Sunan at-Tirmidhi*, Birr, 58
28. *Sunan Abu Dawud*, Adab, 24
29. Ahmad ibn Hanbal, *Musnad*, 11/400
30. *Sunan at-Tirmidhi*, Qiyama, 54
31. *Sunan an-Nasa'i*, Zakah, 72

32. *Sahih Muslim*, Salam, 26

33. At-Targhib wa't-Tarhib, 4/361

34. *Sunan Abu Dawud*, Iman, 7

35. *Sahih al-Bukhari*, Istitaba, 4

36. *Sunan at-Tirmidhi*, Zuhd, 11

37. *Sunan an-Nasa'i*, Jihad, 6

38. *Sunan at-Tirmidhi*, Birr, 3

39. *Sunan Abu Dawud*, Salat, 29

40. *Sahih Muslim*, Iman, 139

41. *Sahih Muslim*, Birr, 6181

42. *Sunan Abu Dawud*, Adab, 7

43. *Sunan Abu Dawud*, 13/5986

44. *Sunan Abu Dawud*, Adab, 35

45. Ajluni, *Kashfu'l-Khafa*, II/102

46. *Sahih al-Bukhari*, Ilm, 69

47. Suyuti, *Jamiu's-Saghir*, 4/3810

48. *Sunan at-Tirmidhi*, 7/155

49. *Sahih Muslim*, Iman, 164

50. *Sahih al-Bukhari*, Adab, 96

51. *Fayzu'l-Qadir*, 188/3

52. *Sunan Abu Dawud*, 36, 4900

53. *Sahih al-Bukhari*, Ar-Riqaq, 421

54. Tabarani, *Al-Mujamu'l-Awsat*, 1/275

55. *An-Nawawi*, 32

56. *Sunan at-Tirmidhi*, Iman, 12

57. *Sunan an-Nasa'i*, Zakah, 72

58. *Sahih al-Bukhari*, Salat, 88

59. *Sunan Abu Dawud*, Tibb, 11

60. *Sunan at-Tirmidhi*, Qiyama, 60

61. *Sahih al-Bukhari*, Iman, 32

62. *Sunan at-Tirmidhi*, Birr, 60

63. *Sunan at-Tirmidhi*, Birr, 55

64. *Sunan at-Tirmidhi*, Birr, 55

65. Ajluni, *Kashfu'l-Khafa*, II/31

66. *Sahih al-Bukhari*, Fadailu'l-Qur'an, 21

67. *Sunan at-Tirmidhi*, Qiyama, 49
68. Suyuti, *Jamiu's-Saghir*, 5180
69. *Sahih al-Bukhari*, Janaiz, 1
70. *Sahih Muslim*, Masajid, 282
71. *Sahih Muslim*, Salah, 13
72. *Bayhaqi*, Shuabu'l-Iman, 2
73. *Sunan ibn Majah*, Taharat, 4
74. *Sunan at-Tirmidhi*, Fadailu'l-Qur'an, 13
75. Ahmad ibn Hanbal, *Musnad*, 1/73
76. *Sahih al-Bukhari*, Ilm, 71
77. Tabarani, *Al-Mujamul Kabir*, 25/7
78. *Sunan ibn Majah*, Muqaddima, 17
79. *Sunan at-Tirmidhi*, 41/2
80. *Majmau'z-Zawaid wa Manbau'l-Fawaid*, 1/122
81. *Sunan at-Tirmidhi*, Ilm, 2
82. *At-Targhib wa't-Tarhib*, I, 112
83. *Sunan ibn Majah*, Muqaddima, 3
84. Ajluni, *Kashfu'l-Khafa*, II/265
85. *Sahih Muslim*, Dhikr, 38
86. Tabarani, *Al-Mujamul Kabir*, I/259
87. *Sunan at-Tirmidhi*, Birr, 40
88. *Sunan at-Tirmidhi*, Birr, 40
89. *Sunan Abu Dawud*, Adab, 36
90. *Sahih Muslim*, Iman, 186
91. *Sahih Muslim*, Birr, 6210
92. Malik, *Muwatta*, Husnu'l-Khuluq, 16
93. *Sahih Muslim*, Imara, 133
94. *Sahih al-Bukhari*, Iman, 32
95. *Sunan at-Tirmidhi*, Tibb, 35
96. *Sunan at-Tirmidhi*, Birr, 16
97. *Sunan at-Tirmidhi*, Birr, 16
98. *Sunan at-Tirmidhi*, Birr, 75
99. *Sahih Muslim*, Birr, 6218
100. *Sahih al-Bukhari*, Adab, 27